SQUADRONS!

No. 57

THE DOUGLAS
SBD
- NEW ZEALAND AND FRANCE -

PHIL H. LISTEMANN

ISBN: 979-1096490-98-1

Copyright

© 2023 Philedition - Phil Listemann

Colour profiles: Gaetan Marie/Bravo Bravo Aviation

The Douglas SBD

The Douglas Dauntless was developed from the Northrop BT-1 as the XBT-2 and was soon redesignated XSBD-1. Modified with some improvements, the SBD-1 was introduced into service in 1940, with 54 being built for the US Marine Corps (USMC). The Dauntless was an all-metal, single-engine monoplane designed to carry out either dive bombing or scout work from aircraft carriers or land bases.

The SBD-1 was followed by the improved -2, of which 87 were delivered between December 1940 and May 1941, but it was the next production version, the SBD-3, that made the Dauntless the backbone of US Navy (USN) attack squadrons for the next two years of the Pacific war. The SBD-3 was the first fully combat-worthy Dauntless and introduced several refinements, including improved armament. Introduced in March 1941, it took part in the theatre's major battles of 1942 and, in all, 585 had been delivered by October 1942. At that time, it was replaced on the production lines by the SBD-4, a version that introduced a new 24-volt electrical system and other refinements. The 780 -4s were built in less than six months, the last being accepted by the Navy in February 1943.

The main production version, the SBD-5, had yet to come. The first delivery took place on 21 February 1943 and was followed by 2,963 more before March 1944, a production and delivery rate indicative of America's increasing industrial capability. Many improvements were again introduced, like a more powerful engine (up rated from 1,000 hp to 1,200 hp). The increased power enabled the offensive load to grow to a maximum of 2,250 pounds. A final version was produced, the -6, with an engine rated at 1,350 hp but the expected increase in performance did not eventuate and only 450 had been built by the summer of 1944. Nevertheless, the Dauntless had already become obsolete by 1943. It remained in front-line service because the introduction of its successor, the Curtiss SB2C Helldiver, was delayed and Japanese air activity from mid-1943 had decreased, allowing the relatively slow and lightly armed Dauntless a better chance of survival.

The Douglas Dauntless remains one of the major types that fought the war in the Pacific, it achieved no such fame in other theatres. It was gradually overshadowed by other types after 1943 but soldiered on until 1945, mainly with USMC units. Its land-based version, the A-24 Banshee, saw little active service.

A USMC SBD-5 returning from a mission over Rabaul in 1944, during the time the New Zealanders were flying their tour. By that time, the USMC was the principal user of the Dauntless as the USN was replacing the type with Curtiss SB2Cs.

Dauntless for New Zealand

As a loyal member of the British Commonwealth, New Zealand had dispatched a considerable number of Army and Air Force personnel to bolster Britain's perilous position in the Middle East and elsewhere during 1940–41. However, after Japan's December 1941 attack on Pearl Harbor, and rapid advance to within striking distance of Australia, New Zealand suddenly found itself dangerously close to the front line.

Despite only having a population of two million during the Second World War, New Zealand was ready to play its part, but was woefully short of modern aircraft. Improvements began when the Royal New Zealand Air Force (RNZAF) was integrated into American South Pacific Command (SOPAC) and deliveries of modern US aircraft commenced – some diverted from British orders.

Within a year, the number of RNZAF squadrons had increased sevenfold and, by the end of 1944, 80% of the RNZAF home-based squadrons had been transferred to offensive operations in the SW Pacific Theatre. Twenty-eight squadrons saw active service in the Pacific before the war ended. Unlike other Allied air forces, the RNZAF received most for its Lend-Lease equipment directly from USN inventory. Indeed, requisitions depended on the concurrence of the local Allied Forces Commander; for the RNZAF, this meant Rear Admiral Ghormley USN.

As the RNZAF units were to fight alongside USMC units flying SBDs, an order for 120 A-24Bs (42-54766–54885), the Army version of the Dauntless, was cancelled in January 1944 and replaced by SBDs. Hence, the US Navy, US Marines, the RNZAF, and the French Air Force in 1944–45, were the only Allied air arms to fly the Dauntless in combat.

The idea of equipping the RNZAF with Dauntless dive bombers was first mooted in February 1943. At that time, the Allied forces under the command of General MacArthur were firmly established on the island of Bougainville and in the western half of New Britain – positions which allowed the heavily defended Japanese base at Rabaul to be attacked from both the east and the west. However, despite a prolonged and intensive bombing campaign throughout 1943, Rabaul, although weakened, remained a formidable fortress.

Since a direct assault would require massive sea and land forces, and could result in heavy casualties, the decision was taken, in early 1944, to step up the air campaign even further before committing ground troops. The RNZAF offered to provide additional squadrons and, under the original plan, Nos. 25, 26, 27 and 28 were to be equipped with the Dauntless. In the event, only No. 25 Squadron used the type operationally as more modern types became available.

The RNZAF used three variants of the Dauntless: the SBD-3 and -4 for training, all on loan from the US Marines; and the SBD-5, which was used on operations by 25 Squadron. The 18 SBD-3s received the serials **NZ5001–5018**, the 27 SBD-4s **NZ5019–5045**, and the 23 SBD-5s **NZ5046–5068**.

Douglas SBD-3 BuNo 4549 with the temporary RNZAF serial NZ208 painted on the rear fuselage. A few weeks later, this aircraft crashed, fortunately without injury to the pilot.

Victories - confirmed or probable claims: -

First operational sortie:
24.03.44
Last operational sortie:
17.05.44

Number of sorties: 530

Total aircraft written-off: 10

Aircraft lost on operations: 5
Aircraft lost in accidents: 5

Squadron code letters:

-

COMMANDING OFFICERS				
S/L Theodore J. MacL. DE LANGE	NZ1060	RNZAF	...	...

SQUADRON USAGE

Number 25 Squadron RNZAF was formed specifically to fly one type of aircraft, the Douglas SBD Dauntless. It was planned to form more squadrons to fly the type but, in the end, 25 Squadron became the only operator. No. 26 Squadron was formed in October 1943 for this purpose but was finally disbanded in January 1944 without having received any aircraft. Operating alongside US Army Air Force and Marine Corps units, 25 completed one operational tour against one major target, Rabaul, making this squadron unique in RNZAF history.

Formed on 31 July 1943, at Seagrove near Auckland, No. 25 Squadron was immediately allocated 12 aircrews and a handful of ground staff under the command of S/L T.J. McLean de Lange. It was initially equipped with nine war-weary ex-USMC SBD-3s and -4s to bring the squadron up to an operational standard. The nine SBD-3s were on loan from Marine Air Group 14 (MAG-14) of the USMC, then based at Seagrove for a period of rest and recuperation. The aircraft were that worn out it took a full week's work before the squadron could get its first SBD airborne. In addition, spares were in short supply and several machines had to be cannibalised, with the help of MAG-14 mechanics, to restore the remainder to flying condition. Maintenance

Squadron Leader T.J. McLean de Lange, CO of No. 25 Squadron, in NZ5057, with his air gunner, F/O L.T. Sewell. Born in India, de Lange was educated in England before moving to New Zealand. He served as a regular officer with the RNZAF from January 1938 to February 1966, retiring with the rank of air commodore. For his outstanding command of the only dive-bombing squadron in the RNZAF, he was awarded the DFC in September 1944. Note the personal insignia chosen by the crew. On the right, ahead of the cockpit, the 25 Sqn crest has been applied.

Some New Zealand pilots and air gunners posing in front of an ex-USMC Dauntless at Seagrove. From left to right, are believed to be: Flight Sergeants N.L. Kelly and B.E. Cullen, F/O G.C. Howie, Flight Sergeants J.S.R. Robertson, O.E. Watson, L.H. Jolly and N.G. Silver, P/O G.H. Grey, F/O F.G. McKenzie and P/O G.H. French. Graham Howie was killed in a Corsair crash (NZ5394) on 13 June 1945 while serving with No. 16 Squadron RNZAF in the South Pacific.

problems continued to hamper training, with a 40% serviceability rate being the norm! The squadron's requests for better aircraft were finally answered at the end of September when the number of SBDs was increased to 17. Eighteen aircraft were delivered (RNZAF serials NZ205–NZ222), followed by a further batch in November 1943 (NZ5019–NZ5027). Dauntless NZ211 crashed during a training flight on 13 September near Waiuku, killing both the pilot, F/O W.D. McJannet and gunner, Sgt Douglas M.J. Cairns. Despite being struck off charge, NZ211 was subsequently renumbered NZ5007. By August, these aircraft began to receive temporary RNZAF serial numbers (NZ205–NZ222) but by late November or early December had been allocated full serials (NZ5001–NZ5018) when this batch was officially placed under RNZAF authority. At this time, many were painted in similar colours, but with the addition of blue/white/blue RNZAF roundels without white bars in six positions. Those on the fuselage sides had a yellow outer ring as per contemporary RAF fuselage roundels. Fin flashes do not appear to have been added to the aircraft at this time, but the last number of the serial was added in white to the fin and the engine cowling of most aircraft.

Training continued for the rest of the year and, bit by bit, a full complement of aircrew was transferred into the squadron. None of the pilots had any experience flying dive bombers. The first batch had come from Army Co-operation squadrons, or second-line units, and were later joined by pilots fresh from flying school. As for the air gunners, most had arrived from Canada where they had been sent for training under the Empire Air Training Scheme; others were assigned from bomber and coastal patrol squadrons for a new operational tour. After an intensive ground course, flight training commenced. To convert to the Dauntless, pilots had to complete a minimum of 60 hours. The programme included dive-bombing practice, a hair-raising experience for the crews, especially the rear gunner who had to sit with his back to the target in a dive at 75 degrees from the horizontal. Alternative modes of attack were the 'semi-vertical' dive at 45 degrees without the perforated trailing-edge airbrakes extended, and the low-level bombing run between 500/1,500 feet.

In addition, there was live-firing practice for both pilot and air gunner, formation flying and day/night navigation exercises. To mark the completion of their training, a formation of 18 aircraft flew over Auckland on the morning of 16 January 1944. At the time,

For 25 Sqn crews, training on the type began with war-weary SBD-3s like this one, NZ5006, repainted with RNZAF roundels. Below NZ5003 and NZ5005.

The other sub-type used by the New Zealanders was the -4. Above, NZ5024, and, below, NZ5025.

Three SDB-3s (NZ5001, NZ5013 and NZ5014) in formation over the New Zealand countryside. By late 1943, the Dauntless was clearly obsolete which is why only one RNZAF squadron eventually operated the type. Better aircraft were already available to the Allies by then, like the Corsair and Avenger, versatile types the New Zealanders were soon to receive.

this was the largest formation of aircraft ever seen over the city. All personnel were then dispatched to Swanson for infantry weapons training and a course in jungle warfare/survival. There was more to come – operational training under tropical conditions at Palikulo airbase on the island of Espiritu Santo in the New Hebrides (now Vanuatu). The ground echelon (No. 25 Servicing Unit) had been sent ahead to prepare for the squadron's arrival. On 30 January, the aircrews of 25 Squadron left New Zealand aboard a No. 40 Squadron Lockheed Lodestar and Douglas Dakota, arriving at Palikulo nine hours later where they found a line-up of 27 newer, but still worn, ex-USMC SBD-4s to replace the worn out -3s left in New Zealand.

The next day, operational training resumed – more dive-bombing practice and live gunnery exercises, formation and instrument flying. On 11 February, during an instrument-flying session, the squadron lost its first aircraft when SBD-4 NZ5037, flown by F/O A. Moore and F/Sgt J.K. Munro, went missing. Despite widespread searches over the following days, neither the aircraft nor crew were found. More than 40 years later, in 1987, the wreck of the missing SBD was discovered 50 kilometres from Santo. There was no trace of the crew. The aircraft was subsequently salvaged and preserved as a museum exhibit. Training continued throughout February, culminating in mock sorties with USMC units (MAG-11, MAG-12 and MAG-21) where the New Zealanders were only a small part of formations that, at times, numbered over 100 aircraft. Towards the end of the month, 25 Squadron began to receive brand-new SBD-5s to replace their second-hand SBD-4s. These were from Marine Corps stocks (NZ5046–NZ5063) and were operated from 19 February in Marine Corps markings. By 25 February, they had been repainted with RNZAF roundels in four positions and RNZAF serial numbers. All appeared to have the large pneumatic tailwheel fitted to land-based USMC aircraft. The old machines were handed back to the Americans at the beginning of March. From that moment on, training was over and 25 Squadron was considered combat ready. Its first op had been scheduled for the end of February, but this was postponed until 22 March because the squadron's forward base at Piva on Bougainville was under repeated bombardment from Japanese artillery. Apart from a few familiarisation flights, there was very little activity at Palikulo while the squadron waited for the ground situation to be resolved.

On the morning of 22 March, the order came through to pack up and head for Piva via Henderson Field on Guadalcanal – a long detour south across open sea. The squadron flew the first leg in two echelons of nine aircraft, each led by a Lockheed PV-1 from No. 9 Squadron. After a flight lasting five hours, all aircraft reached Henderson Field but, on landing, F/O B.N. Graham swerved off the runway and collided with a petrol bowser, writing off NZ5055. The following day, the first nine aircraft, led by S/L de Lange, reached Piva without incident, with the second group arriving on 24 March. Soon after landing, de Lange set about organising an operational sortie. This was a fairly timid artillery spotting exercise. The first aircraft (NZ5049) piloted by F/O L.A. McLellan-

Symonds took off at 0545, followed an hour later by the squadron commander himself and his rear gunner, F/O Sewell. The CO was the first to come back at 0825, McLellan-Symonds landing 40 minutes later without incident. At 0950, six aircraft were provided as part of a force of 18 SBDs and nine TBFs (Grumman Avengers) for a strike on beach and inland targets at Tavera. Only four NZ aircraft, led by F/O F.G. McKenzie and his gunner in NZ5061, took off on the mission but all dropped their bombs in the target area. In the early afternoon, five aircraft were included in a force of 18 SBDs and three TBFs for a strike just outside the airfield perimeter. This attack, led by the B Flight commander, F/L T.R.F. Johnson, was unique for two reasons. First, it was possible for the ground crew, who had just refuelled and rearmed the aircraft, to see bombs falling from the same aircraft as they attacked Japanese positions. Secondly, the leading American SBD carried an officer of Fiji's 1st Battalion as an observer. This officer, Lieutenant Viggers, advised the formation leader on which positions to attack. Later, at 1710, F/L Johnson was airborne again, leading six aircraft this time, and, with Viggers as observer, attacked the same target. As a result of this attack, the squadron suffered its first aircraft damage. Flight Sergeants N.L. Kelly and B.E. Cullen brought back NZ5062 with a bullet hole in the rudder (this aircraft survived the war and is regularly flown in California). Including the two artillery spotting flights performed at noon, the squadron performed 19 sorties that day, a good start for the Kiwis. The following day, two strikes were carried out on local gun positions, both took place before midday. In each case, the strike force was nine SBDs and six TBFs; the squadron provided all the SBDs. In the second strike at least, the TBFs were from No. 30 Squadron RNZAF. Results were quite successful and at least one gun emplacement was completely destroyed. The day ended with two artillery spotting flights carried out by mixed crews of Kiwi pilot (Sergeants C.G.W. Kuhn and A.C.L. Forsberg) and USMC observer on board two USMC SBDs ('181' and '177'). March 26 should have been squadron's first long-range strike, but it became an abortive one. The target was Kavieng airfield, New Ireland, and the force from Piva was 36 SBDs, 12 TBFs and eight escorts. In addition, 18 SBDs and 12 TBFs based at Green Island were to join the attack. The squadron provided 12 aircraft but, after leaving Green Island, these, plus six American SBDs failed to rendezvous with the rest of the strike force due to poor weather conditions and returned to Green Island after 2.5 hours flying. After a brief time on the ground, they flew back to Piva. The next day, at 0850, a strike force of 28 SBDs, 22 TBFs and eight escorts was airborne for a strike on Rabaul. The squadron contribution was six aircraft, led by A Flight leader, F/L J.W. Edwards, but F/Sgt Kelly and his gunner (NZ5062) had to return owing to fuel trouble. The target was an ammunition dump and supply area at Talili Bay. The strike was successful as a large amount of damage was caused. Later in the afternoon, a force of 12 SBDs and nine TBFs attacked Japanese positions three miles inland from the mouth of the Maririci River. Because of dense foliage, results were difficult to assess. Half of the SBDs were from 25, led this time by the other flight leader, F/L Johnson. Lakunai airfield runway and gun positions were the targets for a Rabaul strike force of 36 SBDs, 24 TBFs and eight escorts on 28 March. The squadron provided 11 aircraft, led by the CO, but two of these aborted (Sgt Kuhn and F/Sgt M. Small – NZ5053 – and Sgt P.R.B. Symonds and F/Sgt B. Boden – NZ5049) because of engine and instrument trouble. Anti-aircraft (AA) fire was moderate to intense but not very accurate. NZ5046 (F/O

Last check before take-off for NZ5056, the regular mount of Flight Sergeants C.N. O'Neill and D.W. Gray.

As flight commander, F/L T.R.F. Johnson (left) played a major role, often leading the Kiwis in combat. F/Sgt R.J. Howell, his air gunner, is on the right. Like Graham Howie, Johnson started another tour with No. 16 Squadron RNZAF in the South Pacific, but was killed on 15 January 1945, flying Corsair NZ5283. He was one of eight Kiwi Corsair pilots lost that day, one of the blackest days for the RNZAF in the Pacific. *(JR Cullen via P. Sortehaug)*

L.H.F. Brown and F/Sgt G.D. Ashworth) came home with several machine gun holes in the tailplane. The next day was a quiet one for the Kiwis and only six aircraft, led by F/L Johnson (part of a force of 27 SBDs, 18 TBFs and eight escorts), were airborne for a strike on the Vunapope area. The Kiwi aircraft attacked automatic AA positions, scoring three damaging hits. On 30 March, gun positions around Vunakanau airfield received attention from 36 SBDs, 24 TBFs and their ubiquitous eight escorts. It was not a very successful mission. The SBDs were hampered by cloud which partially obscured the target and only ten hits were recorded. Also, bombs carried by two RNZAF aircraft failed to release. Although AA fire was almost non-existent, small arms fire was responsible for a shattered canopy on NZ5050 (P/O G.H. Cray and F/Sgt F.D. Bell). An American SBD was successfully ditched on the way to the target and the crew rescued by a Catalina. This was the first mission in which 25 Squadron led the SBD force; 12 aircraft were provided under the command of S/L de Lange. On the last day of the month, the squadron's 12 aircraft, under the command of F/L Edwards, joined with three other squadrons to provide 54 SBDs for a strike on the gun positions around the airfield at Lakunai. The force, including 18 TBFs and eight escorts, took off at 1000 for an attack timed for noon. The results were fairly successful; the New Zealanders scoring five of the 15 hits recorded.

So far, the first operations had been carried without major incident, but things changed in April. On the first day of that month, the Kiwis were on duty again. The supply and bivouac area on the Maririci River was again the target. During mid-morning, with de Lange in the lead, and again in mid-afternoon but led by Edwards, a force of six Kiwi SBDs and six TBFs struck the area. As with previous strikes, the results were hard to assess; the afternoon strike was hampered by showery weather. The following day, 54 SBDs, 24 TBFs and eight escorts combined with 12 aircraft from Green Island to attack gun positions at Rabaul. Cloud over the target forced the mission to attack the secondary target which was Raluana Point; buildings, gun positions and the barge area in Karavia Bay were all struck with moderate success. AA was light and inaccurate. This strike was the first in which the SBDs carried .2 × 125-lb fragmentation clusters. NZ5054 (Flight Sergeants L.H. Jolly and T.E. Price) and NZ5059 (Sgt PR.B. Symonds and F/Sgt B. Boden), both had hang-ups of these clusters which exploded during the landing at Piva. Jolly was unhurt but the other three men were all injured. Both aircraft were burnt beyond repair; this was the last time SBDs carried that type of armament. On 3 April, de Lange led 60 SBDs, including 12 aircraft from the squadron, on a strike on Vunakanau. Also taking part were 24 TBFs and eight escorts. Cloud cover of 70% made accurate bombing difficult and, although some hits were recorded, results were generally not assessable. Some of the aircraft attacked the airfield at Tobera in lieu of their assigned target. One squadron aircraft (NZ5053) did not take part in the strike because of engine trouble. April 4 was a very sad day for 25 Squadron, as it lost its first aircrew. In the morning F/O L.A .McLellan-Symonds in an American aircraft, '161', and Flying Officers B.N. Graham and G.C .Howie in NZ5048,

Johnson and Howell heading for another target in their usual aircraft, NZ5049.

flew via Munda (near Ondonga) to Henderson Field, Guadalcanal, in order to pick up two other aircraft. The aircraft were in US markings and codes, McLellan-Symonds piloting '176', Graham in '14' and Howie in NZ5048. They took off at 1410 and shortly afterwards landed at Russell Island to refuel before flying direct to Piva. On the way to Piva, they experienced radio transmission difficulties between themselves and, on ETA, they could see no land. The weather started to deteriorate; darkness was not far off when the wingmen recognised the coast of New Britain. Because of the radio problem, they could not let McLellan-Symonds know where they were; he thought he was still lost. They turned back and were headed for Green Island when, inexplicably, McLellan-Symonds broke formation. Although Air-Sea Rescue received a transmission of an intended ditching, he was never seen again. After the war, it was discovered he had been captured by the Japanese and held in the PoW camp at Tunnel Hill Road where he died from blood poisoning on 25 May 1944. The other two aircraft landed safely at Green Island about an hour after dark. After a day without operations due to poor weather, the squadron was back at work on 6 April. Vunakanau was again the target for a force of 66 SBDs (12 from the squadron led by F/L Edwards), 24 TBFs and eight escorts; cloud intervened again, so the force attacked the secondary target, the Talili Bay supply area. Results were fair and many direct hits were reported on buildings, gun positions, and one on an oil storage tank. Moderate AA fire caused no damage to the SBDs. The next day the New Zealanders only provided six aircraft for a strike on Rabaul by 42 SBDs, 36 TBFs and the usual escorts. The target was gun positions in the Talili Bay area; the result was three guns destroyed and six damaged. On 8 April, 48 SBDs, 17 TBFs and escorts struck gun positions along the ridge near Rataval. Out of 14 hits reported by the SBDs, the NZ aircraft accounted for five. AA fire was fairly intense and accurate but, apart from a few small holes, the SBDs got off lightly. While this was going on, five other Kiwi SBDs were in a force of 12 which struck gun positions 1,000 yards west of the Mamagata River. Two aircraft scored direct hits on a pill box; one of these was the CO's aircraft, NZ5057. The following day, the Japanese received a visit from 60 SBDs, 24 TBFs and six escorts, led by de Lange and 11 other squadron aircraft for a very successful attack on Vunakanau gun positions. Known positions gave little AA opposition but four new positions were found putting up an intense barrage, damaging eight of the Dauntlesses. NZ5051 (F/L Edwards and F/Sgt L.A. Hoppe) had its starboard wing and tailplane extensively damaged and the radio aerial shot away, while NZ5048 (F/O Howie and F/Sgt J.S.R. Robertson) sported a hole in the rear fuselage. On the way to the target, a 'Zeke', or possibly a 'Hamp', was seen off Cape St George. On 10 April, an approach at 12,500 feet from the south-west was made on Raluana Point and Vunapope. The SBDs dived 9,000 feet, released bombs at 2,500 feet and leveled off at 1,500, strafing islands in St George's Channel on the way out. Moderate AA fire greeted the aircraft and NZ5047 (F/O Brown and F/Sgt Ashworth), NZ5049 (F/L Johnson and F/Sgt Howell) and NZ5061 (F/O

On 14 May 1944, twelve 25 Sqn SBDs were sent to strike the Vunakanau runway with 12 USMC SBDs and 24 TBFs. Above, the SBDs taxiing with Sergeant C.W. Kuhn and Flight Sergeant M. Small in the forefront on NZ5053 and below the SBDs on the way to the target.
The three nearest Dauntlesses are NZ5049 (F/L T.R.F. Johnson and F/Sgt R.J. Howell), NZ5068 on his left (F/O A.W.B. Hayman and Sgt D.H. Wilkie) and, on his right, NZ5065 (F/Sgt W.O. Nicholson and F/Sgt R.W. Cullen).

McKenzie/P/O G.H. French) all received holes in various control surfaces. The squadron provided 12 aircraft, one of which aborted the mission early (NZ5053 – Sgt Kuhn and F/Sgt Small), but most of the rest struck the Vunapope target. Eighteen TBFs co-ordinated their attack and both targets were fairly well covered with bombs. A possible 'Hamp' was again seen off Cape St George and, on the run into the target, two NZ gunners, F/Sgt D.W. Gray (NZ5056) and F/Sgt T.E. Price (NZ5060) sighted four 'Zekes' over Vunakanau. The rising sun markings were clearly visible as the fighters sat just above and 1,000 yards to port of the SBD formation. After about half a minute, they broke away with no attempt to intercept the Allied force. On 11, 12 and 13 April, the Kiwis supplied 12 aircraft and several hits were confirmed during each raid. The next day, two aircraft were detailed as spares for a strike on Vunakanau. In the event, their services were called upon. Among the crewmen were the newcomers F/L J.R. Penniket and F/O J.H. Brady who had arrived from Guadalcanal on the 12th to gain combat experience. Penniket was a potential CO of the proposed new dive-bombing squadron, No. 26. Even then, though, the formation of this unit had already been postponed. A small force of three Kiwi SBDs and three TBFs attacked coastal guns at Buka Passage. The guns were not deterred by the bombing but ceased firing after strafing runs were made. NZ5065 (Flight Sergeants W.O. Nicholson and R.W. Cullen) was holed by shrapnel in the port wing and starboard tank. The targets for 15 April were gun positions surrounding Lakunai which received a pounding from 48 SBDs; the runway was well covered by 36 TBFs. Squadron Leader de Lange led the SBDs with the usual NZ contribution of 12 SBDs while eight escort fighters accompanied the bombers. NZ5064 (F/O B.N. Graham and Sgt O.E. Watson) and NZ5053 (Kuhn and Small) were both damaged by explosive shells. The following day, 52 SBDs carried a different bomb load of one 500-lb and two 250-lb bombs. Targets were gun positions and the runway at Vunakanau. Many hits were scored, including 96 on the runway. Eighteen TBFs attacked the same targets and the Kiwis again provided 12 SBDs. One 250-lb bomb fell off NZ5057, the CO's aircraft, during take-off; fortunately, it did not explode but certainly provided a heart-stopping moment. Bomb loads were mixed on 17 April with two of the 12 Kiwi SBDs reverted to carrying a single 1,000-lb bomb. Forty-eight SBDs, 30 TBFs and eight escorts comprised the force which struck gun positions and the runway at Lakunai. The strike was a success, but AA was fairly intense and NZ5050, which was last seen at high speed over the target area, did not rendezvous afterwards. It was believed to have been shot down with its crew, P/O Cray and F/Sgt Bell reported missing (Bell was on his second tour). Another SBD, NZ5058 (Sgt Forsberg and F/Sgt E.G. Leatham) received extensive damage in this raid, so much that the aircraft was considered beyond economical repair and written off.

The squadron was airborne over the next two days, providing six and nine aircraft, but bad weather prevented any take off on the 20th and 21st. On 22 April, weather again took a hand and prevented a force of 54 SBDs, 24 TBFs and eight fighters from attacking either their primary (Vunakanau) or secondary (Lakunai) targets. As a result, Rapopo Airfield was extensively damaged and, of the 12 NZ aircraft leading the strike (led by the CO), 11 reported direct hits on the runway while the other one hit a building. AA fire was meagre. Ops on the two following days were also cancelled due to bad weather and it was only on the 25th that another mission could be carried out. That day, escorted by eight fighters, 48 SBDs and 18 TBFs bombed gun positions in the vicinity of Lakunai airfield. The squadron provided its usual 12 aircraft (led by F/L Edwards); one of the SBDs, NZ5061 (F/L Penniket and F/O Brown),

No. 25 SU personnel preparing SBD-4 NZ5034 for another training flight at Espiritu Santo (New Hebrides) in February 1944.

Dauntless NZ5064 flown by F/O F.G. McKenzie and P/O G.H. French. This SBD was a bit peculiar as it had no fin flash and the US white star is still visible under the RNZAF roundel.

brought back a souvenir in the form of a piece of shrapnel stuck in the flaps near the starboard wing root. The following day, the runway at Vunakanau received 62 direct hits from 46 SBDs and 24 TBFs. Ten Kiwi aircraft led the formation (with de Lange in the lead). Two others (NZ5060 and NZ5066) did not take off because of engine trouble. NZ5049 (F/L Johnson and F/Sgt Howell) had its propeller badly damaged by a shell burst and had to land at Green Island. After yet another day grounded by bad weather, the squadron tried to strike Lakunai airfield on the 28th but the formation turned back again due to the weather. Finally, however, weather was on the Allied side on 29 April when 36 SBDs (12 from the squadron), 24 TBFs and four escorting fighters switched their attention to targets on Buka Island. The formation bombed two targets: military barracks at Tahitahi Point and native huts at Lonahan Village. Several direct hits were scored. April ended with 12 sorties flown to provide artillery reconnaissance in the perimeter area.

The first day of May began with local artillery reconnaissance. The next day, in a glide-bombing attack on the runway at Tobera, SBDs alone dropped 100 bombs on the runway. The 12 NZ aircraft led the strike and all but one hit the runway with their load of one 1,000-lb and two 100-lb bombs. On 3 May, Vunakanau was relatively clear of cloud and the force bombed the runway, surrounding buildings, gun positions and even the bridge at the mouth of the Warangoi River. AA damaged several aircraft including NZ5060 (Flight Sergeants Jolly and RF Bailey), NZ5063 (F/L Penniket and F/O Brady) and NZ5066 (Flight Sergeants J.C .Evison and H.A. Sharp). The force consisted of 36 SBDs, 24 TBFs and four escorts, and was led by 25 Squadron aircraft. After an abortive attempt on the 4th, with the mission cancelled because of the weather, six Kiwi SBDs of (led by de Lange) were assigned to attack a heavy AA position near Mt Boeder and the Muguai Mission on the 5th. Because of cloud, Mt Boeder could not be located so all aircraft dropped through a gap in the cloud in the mission area with unobserved results. In the afternoon, a further six, aircraft (led by F/L Johnson) sought out coastal guns and a searchlight near Sorum on the north-east coast of Bougainville. They had a little more success than the morning mission and dropped their bombs on a clearing about three miles south of Sorum. Results were unobserved. The following day, despite a 50-mile weather diversion en route, visibility was unlimited over the supply area at Rataval and 24 SBDs and 18 TBFs, plus four escorts, attacked but with limited success. One exception was F/Sgt C.M. O'Neill and his gunner, F/Sgt D.W. Gray, in NZ5056. One of the leading 12 New Zealand aircraft, he scored a direct hit on a petrol dump. An immense explosion occurred, and a sheet of flame was seen, followed by black smoke billowing to 4,000 feet. The flames died down after five minutes, but the smoke was still visible from 25 miles away. On 7 May, military installations on Bantan Island, South Bougainville, were dive bombed by six aircraft; two US SBDs with photographers on board accompanied them. Extensive cloud hampered the operation. Before the end of the day, the squadron also carried out 12 local artillery reconnaissance sorties. The next

day was not a big one for the New Zealanders, as six aircraft were ordered to bomb and strafe coastal guns at Cape Friendship, South Bougainville. One had to turn back (NZ5052 – Flight Sergeants Jolly and Bailey) with engine trouble; the other five had no luck finding the guns although AA fire was observed. The target area was bombed with no apparent result. TBFs also struck the area about the same time. The next mission came two days later, on 10 May. Back to Lakunai and gun positions close by, and on 'Hospital Ridge'. This time, the barrage of flak was more intense than before. NZ5051, flown by F/L Edwards and his gunner F/Sgt Hoppe – were reportedly hit by flak just after releasing their bomb and crashed into the sea off Great Harbour, killing both crewmen. It was a cruel blow, just a week before the squadron was due to pack its bags. The strike was led by 12 Kiwi aircraft (S/L de Lange), the total force being 18 SBDs, 12 TBFs and four escorts.

The weather over Vunakanau was unsuitable for the mission of 11 May, so the force of 48 SBDs, 24 TBFs and four escorts attacked secondary targets at Tobera and Marawaka (south of Piva). The leading six American SBDs were armed with eight 5-inch rockets each but, in the circumstances, did not use them. The RNZAF SBDs attacked as follows: eight hit the Marawak area; three dropped their bombs on the bridge over the Warangoi River (New Britain); and one, experiencing engine trouble, jettisoned its bomb and landed at Green Island. The next day, targets, all around the Rabaul area, were assigned to a combined force of 48 SBDs and 24 TBFs. Escorting aircraft increased to 12. AA was fairly light and strikes were made in most areas from Talili Bay to beyond Raluana Point. No. 25 Squadron provided its usual 12 aircraft; NZ5067 suffered slight damage (Flight Sergeants Forsberg and Leatham). All aircraft involved landed at Green Island after the attack to refuel and bomb up for another strike on the way home. The targets this time were native villages on the coast south of Sorum where practically all the bombs fell in the target area. After two artillery reconnaissance sorties on the 13th, the New Zealanders took part in another major operation the following day: the runway at Vunakanau and gun positions were bombed by 24 SBDs and 24 TBFs. Half the Dauntlesses were from the squadron, which was leading, and several direct hits were achieved. Just after leaving the target, two gunners saw six Japanese fighters about five miles away. They were doing slow rolls and steep climbing turns and made no attempt to intercept! The two following days, the squadron sent aircraft over North Bougainville and the Tobera area, before the last day of operations on 17 May. Two missions were carried out that day, the last being in the afternoon when five aircraft (one came back early due to mechanical trouble – NZ5052 and Jolly and Bailey again) led by the CO took off to bomb the supply area near Buka airfield. Later, two Kiwi crews flew American SBDs '115' and '110' on reconnaissance sorties over the East Bougainville area.

On 20 May, the surviving aircraft were ferried to Renard Field in the Russell Islands by their crews and handed back to the Marine Corps. Most aircraft had flown about 120 hours and, to the astonishment of the receiving officer, were in 'as-new' condition! This was indeed a tribute to the men of No. 25 Servicing Unit who had toiled away in sometimes atrocious conditions, and with few supplies of spare parts. After eight weeks of almost daily combat, the squadron flew over 530 sorties and 1,500 flying hours on operations. It dropped 280 tons of bombs, fired 108,000 rounds of 0.50-in and 217 rounds of 0.30-in. On the debit side, the squadron lost two aircraft as a direct result of enemy action plus three more while engaged on operations. Despite its many sterling qualities, the SBD was a pre-war design and no longer regarded as a front-line aircraft. The next day, the crews were flown back to Whenuapai in New Zealand in two Dakotas from No. 40 Squadron, where 25 Squadron was disbanded on 19 June. It re-formed at Ardmore on 30 October as a fighter squadron; training commenced on F4U-1 Corsairs.

All the remaining SBD-3s and -4s in New Zealand were used for limited crew training until February 1944; they were then placed in open storage at Hobsonville Airfield. They were sold for scrap in 1948. The surviving Dauntless pilots of 25 Squadron were transferred to the eight RNZAF squadrons equipped with F4U Corsairs and began another operational tour. Two ex-25 Squadron pilots, flying Corsairs, were killed: Johnson and Howie.

F/L J.W. Edwards (right) and W/O L.A. Hoppe in front of their regular mount, NZ5051/Kia Kaha, in which they were killed on 10 May 1944. Note the individual marking and the simplified squadron badge.

KNOWN NUMBER OF SORTIE COMPLETED BY EACH SBD-5

Serial	First sortie	Last sortie	Nb Sortie	Not completed	Op.hours	Comment
NZ5046	24.03.44	16.05.44	30	3	85.2	
NZ5047	24.03.44	15.05.44	34	2	90.6	
NZ5048	24.03.44	17.05.44	40	3	107.1	
NZ5049	24.03.44	17.05.44	23	3	70.7	
NZ5050	24.03.44	17.04.44	15	1	47.1	Lost on its 16th sortie
NZ5051	24.03.44	10.05.44	27	1	77.1	Lost on its 28th sortie
NZ5052	24.03.44	17.05.44	29	4	88.2	
NZ5053	25.03.44	17.05.44	10	3	31.0	
NZ5054	25.03.44	02.04.44	6	1	12.5	Crashed on return
NZ5055	-	-	-	-	-	Crashed on ferry flight
NZ5056	27.03.44	16.05.44	31	2	89.3	
NZ5057	24.03.44	17.05.44	36	1	101.6	
NZ5058	24.03.44	17.04.44	11	2	38.5	
NZ5059	24.03.44	02.04.44	7	1	17.8	Crashed on return
NZ5060	24.03.44	11.05.44	32	2	95.9	
NZ5061	24.03.44	16.05.44	33	3	94.7	
NZ5062	24.03.44	17.05.44	28	3	89.3	
NZ5063	08.04.44	17.05.44	23	1	62.2	
NZ5064	01.04.44	17.05.44	25	1	76.0	
NZ5065	03.04.44	17.05.44	25	1	67.3	
NZ5066	13.04.44	16.05.44	24	3	68.9	
NZ5067	26.04.44	16.05.44	12	-	32.0	
NZ5068	28.04.44	14.05.44	11	-	26.9	

Notes :
Also, two other sorties were performed with a mixed crew NZ/US on USMC aircraft 177 and 181 on 25 March 1944.

SBD-3

NZ Serial	Previous	BuNo	On loan	Wfu
NZ5001	NZ205	06651	03.11.43	Feb-44
NZ5002	NZ206	06652	26.10.43	Feb-44
NZ5003	NZ207	4672	21.10.43	Feb-44
NZ5004	NZ208	4559	03.11.43	Jan-44
NZ5005	NZ209	4585	03.11.43	Feb-44
NZ5006	NZ210	03371	26.10.43	Feb-44
NZ5007	NZ211	03219	?	Sep-43
NZ5008	NZ212	4675	?	Feb-44
NZ5009	NZ213	4652	03.11.43	Feb-44
NZ5010	NZ214	06658	03.11.43	Feb-44
NZ5011	NZ215	03202	14.11.43	Feb-44
NZ5012	NZ216	4645	03.11.43	Feb-44
NZ5013	NZ217	03364	03.11.43	Feb-44
NZ5014	NZ218	03364	03.11.43	Feb-44
NZ5015	NZ219	06649	03.11.43	Feb-44
NZ5016	NZ220	06545	13.11.43	Feb-44
NZ5017	NZ221	03369	03.11.43	Feb-44
NZ5018	NZ222	06519	?	Feb-44

SBD-4

NZ Serial	Previous	BuNo	On loan	Wfu
NZ5019	-	10389	14.11.43	Feb-44
NZ5020	-	10632	14.11.43	Feb-44
NZ5021	-	10508	14.11.43	Feb-44
NZ5022	-	10345	14.11.43	Feb-44
NZ5023	-	10582	14.11.43	Feb-44
NZ5024	-	10539	14.11.43	Feb-44
NZ5025	-	10691	14.11.43	Feb-44
NZ5026	-	10599	13.11.43	Feb-44
NZ5027	-	10583	13.11.43	Feb-44
NZ5028	-	06952	17.12.43	Feb-44
NZ5029	-	10535	17.12.43	Feb-44
NZ5030	-	06744	17.12.43	Feb-44
NZ5031	-	10407	17.12.43	Feb-44
NZ5032	-	10404	17.12.43	Feb-44
NZ5033	-	06740	17.12.43	Feb-44
NZ5034	-	06766	17.12.43	Feb-44
NZ5035	-	06763	17.12.43	Feb-44
NZ5036	-	06815	17.12.43	Feb-44
NZ5037	-	06953	26.12.43	Feb-44
NZ5038	-	10393	26.12.43	Feb-44
NZ5039	-	06931	26.12.43	Feb-44
NZ5040	-	10607	26.12.43	Feb-44
NZ5041	-	06961	30.12.43	Feb-44
NZ5042	-	10384	08.01.44	Feb-44
NZ5043	-	10636	08.01.44	Feb-44
NZ5044	-	06789	26.01.44	Feb-44
NZ5045	-	10500	26.01.44	Feb-44

SBD-5

NZ Serial	BuNo	Returned
NZ5046	36862	20.05.44
NZ5047	36891	20.05.44
NZ5048	36895	20.05.44
NZ5049	36897	20.05.44
NZ5050	36898	-
NZ5051	36908	-
NZ5052	36910	20.05.44
NZ5053	36911	20.05.44
NZ5054	36914	-
NZ5055	36923	-
NZ5056	36924	20.05.44
NZ5057	36925	20.05.44
NZ5058	36928	-
NZ5059	36916	-
NZ5060	28516	20.05.44
NZ5061	28526	20.05.44
NZ5062	28536	20.05.44
NZ5063	10849	20.05.44
NZ5064	54201	20.05.44
NZ5065	54212	20.05.44
NZ5066	28435	20.05.44
NZ5067	10895	20.05.44

An uncomfortable position for SBD-4 NZ5024, after it swung on landing, 15 December 1943 at Seagrove. Except for one fatal accident which cost two lives, training in New Zealand was relatively trouble free. A handful of minor accidents were recorded; NZ5017 on 28.11.43 - damaged by gunfire, NZ5013 on 29.11.43 - engine failure, NZ5026 on 11.12.43 - damaged during gun test and NZ5004 - damaged on landing. At Espiritu Santo, one more minor accident was recorded on 18.02.44 when NZ5029's brakes failed on landing.

Date	Pilot	S/N	Origin	Serial	Code	Fate
02.04.44	F/Sgt Leslie H. **JOLLY**	NZ42410	RNZAF	**NZ5054**	54	-
	F/Sgt Thomas E. **PRICE**	NZ411045	RNZAF			-
	Sgt Peter R.B. **SYMONDS**	NZ424218	RNZAF	**NZ5059**	59	-
	F/Sgt Belie **BODEN**	NZ41303	RNZAF			-
17.04.44	P/O Geoffrey H. **CRAY**	NZ4213648	RNZAF	**NZ5050**	50	†
	F/Sgt Frank D. **BELL**	NZ413244	RNZAF			†
	Sgt Alfred C.L. **FORSBERG**	NZ4212702	RNZAF	**NZ5058**	58	-
	F/Sgt Edward G. **LEATHAM**	NZ413263	RNZAF			-
10.05.44	F/L Jack W. **EDWARDS**	NZ39908	RNZAF	**NZ5051**	51	†
	W/O Louis A. **HOPPE**	NZ415533	RNZAF			†

Total: 5

P/O G.H. Cray and F/Sgt F.D. Bell were the first 25 Sqn members killed in action, believed to have been shot down by anti-aircraft fire.

Date	Pilot	S/N	Origin	Serial	Code	Fate
13.09.43	P/O William D. **MCJANNET**	NZ421249	RNZAF	**NZ211**		†
	Sgt Douglas M.J. **CAIRNS**	NZ422687	RNZAF			†
19.01.44	P/O Roy S. **MCINTOSH**	NZ1911	RNZAF	**NZ5004** [1]		-
11.02.44	P/O Alexander **MOORE**	NZ416523	RNZAF	**NZ5037**		†
	F/Sgt John K. **MUNRO**	NZ417229	RNZAF			†
22.03.44	P/O Bruce N. **GRAHAM**	NZ416109	RNZAF	**NZ5055**		-
	Sgt Olver E. **WATSON**	NZ414365	RNZAF			†
04.04.44	F/O Leslie A. **MCLELLAN-SYMONDS**	NZ401314	RNZAF	**28452** [2]		**PoW/†**

Total: 5

[1] At this time NZ5004 was listed as being with No. 26 Squadron, a unit that was never quite formed. Damage to the aircraft was initially listed as category "C" but later changed to category "E", a write off.

[2] USN aircraft, borrowed

This page and the following, some SBD crews:

Above left, Flying Officer L.H.F. Brown and Flight Sergeant G.D. Ashworth posing in front of their SBD-5, NZ5047/Carborundum Nil Barstardium and above right Flying Officer B.N. Graham and Flight Sergeant O.E. Watson in front of NZ5055, a crew who later flew NZ5064 on which it was applied a very similar personal marking.
Below left, Flight Sergeant L.H. Jolly and T.E. Price (NZ5054/ Homes! The Caper) and right Sergeants C.N. O'Neill and D.W. Gray (NZ5056/Paddys Mistake).

Above left, Flying Officer F.G. MacKenzie and Pilot Officer G.H. French (NZ5061); above right Flight Sergeants N.L. Kelly and B.E. Cullen (NZ5062). Below left, Sergeant P.R.B. Symonds and Flight Sergeant B. Boden (NZ5059); below right Sergeant C.W. Kuhn and Flight Sergeant M. Small (NZ5053).

Above left, Flight Sergeants H. Clark and N.G. Silver (NZ5052); above right Flight Sergeant R.W. Cullen and Sergeant W.O. Nicholson. Below Flight Sergeant A.C.L. Fosberg and Warrant Officer E.G. Leatham (NZ5058).

Under the wartime system each operational Squadron had a Servicing Unit (SU) which was often, though not always, numbered the same. This unit took care of all but the major overhaul and repairs a squadron's aircraft might require. In the case of No. 25 Squadron the maintenance personnel were initially posted into the Squadron itself. Many were from the Army Co-op Squadron at Onerahi and some already had experience servicing US SBDs in the Pacific. Faced with the formidable task of keeping the wellworn SBD-3s serviceable for training flights the men set to work with few and poor facilities at first.

On 23 November No. 25 Squadron lost all its maintenance staff who were posted to the newly formed No. 25 SU under the command of Flying Officer A. Hamilton. This of course was a paper transaction and made little difference to the daily tasks of the men. With the end of training in sight, two-thirds of the SU, A & B Flights, embarked for Santo on board USS OCTANS, on 6 December, arriving at their new Base Depot on the 12th. Their task was to prepare the SBDs for the Squadron's arrival. C Flight moved to Santo by air in January 1944. On completion of the aircrew operational training at Santo, the SU moved by ship to Piva and set up camp ready for the Squadron's arrival. They arrived at Piva on 9 March to find the area subjected to continual shelling by day and night. In spite of this the men worked towards the successful completion of their task and were ready for the SBD-5s when they arrived. The immediate launching into operations of the aircraft gave a large boost to the morale of the SU. Not only could they see their aircraft in action, but after weeks of shelling, when they were powerless to hit back, they could now retaliate.

Over the next eight weeks the SU members worked tirelessly to keep the aircraft serviceable. Only once did they fail to provide the number of aircraft asked for - they were one short - after a mission when one aircraft was shot down and another eight damaged. Throughout the operational tour the overall serviceability rate was 95%, an exceptionally high figure. The CO and aircrew had (and still have) nothing but praise for the efforts of the men of No. 25 SU. Eloquent testimony was contained in the remarks of the American commander who accepted the aircraft when they were handed back after the tour. His remarks were to the effect that as far as he was concerned the Kiwis had handed back brand new aircraft! Flight time on each one was around 120 hours. The SU remained to service other RNZAF aircraft after the departure of the Squadron, as SU's remained in the forward area for longer periods than the Squadrons. They were relieved by personnel rotation rather than the block movement common to aircrew.

Dauntlesses of No. 25 Squadron and the USMC ready to take-off for another mission. In the foreground is NZ5062 flown by Flight Sergeants N.L. Kelly and B.E. Cullen. Just ahead is another SBD from the Squadron with an extra-large fuselage.

WITH THE BRITISH

The Royal Navy acquired a small number of SBD-5, essentially to carry out trials of the DBS-1 bombsight which was also fitted to the Dauntless' successor, the Curtiss SB2C Helldiver, which was expected to enter Fleet Air Arm service. The first arrived in the UK in November 1943. In all, nine flew under British markings.

JS997   ex-BuNo 36022   Accepted USN Sep-43 and served between November 1943 and August 1945 at least.

JS998   ex-BuNo 36023   Accepted USN Sep-43. Stored at 51 MU as spare aircraft but eventually was used at SF Eastleigh between March 1945 and July 1946.

JS999   ex-BuNo 36456   Accepted USN Nov-43. Stored at 51 MU at first then used for various test flights at Farnborough between March and July 1944. Then issued to No. 787 Sqn. Suffered an accident on 31.07.44 following an undercarriage failure. Not repaired.

JT923   ex-BuNo 54191   Accepted USN Jan-44. Initially stored then issued to SF Eastleigh by August 1945. Suffered an engine failure on take-off on 20.06.46 and crashed. The aircraft was declared not repairable.

JT924   ex-BuNo 54192   Accepted USN Jan-44. Stored at No. 51 MU then went to the RAF in April 1945. Used until Feb-46 then stored at No. 34 MU. SOC 15.10.46.

JT925   ex-BuNo 54193   Accepted USN Jan-44. Stored at No. 5 MU, then went to the RAF in April 1945. Used until Feb-46 then stored at No. 34 MU. SOC 15.10.46.

JT926   ex-BuNo 54194   Accepted USN Jan-44. Stored at No. 51 MU, then to RAF on 08.06.44 at Handling Squadron. Later stored at No. 15 MU. SOC 30.03.45.

JT927   ex-BuNo 54195   Accepted USN Jan-44. Stored at No. 51 MU then to No. 700 Sqn between December 44 and February 1946.

JT928   ex-BuNo 54196   Accepted USN Jan-44. Stored at No. 51 MU, then used at the RAE between 13.08.44 and 02.10.44 when it was issued to No. 787 Sqn, but returned to the RAE on 10.10.44, then back to 787 Sqn on 14.10.44. Again with RAE between 09.12.44 and 29.03.46, then stored and probably SOC soon afterwards.

A further allocation of fourteen more aircraft was cancelled, and the serial numbers JT929-JT962 which had been reserved for further aircraft, to a total of 43, were not used.

Douglas SBD-5 JS997 seen at Boscombe Down in December 1943 for trials of its dive-bombing sight.

A line-up of French Douglas A-24s. France was unique in having both variants of the type in its inventory. Indeed, France was allotted 100 A-24s, 98 of which are known to have been delivered.

With the French

The French were unusual users of the Dauntless. When they re-joined the Allies in 1943, the question of re-arming their armed forces was raised, not only for the Air Force but also for the Navy. Indeed, before the war, the French had an aircraft carrier so the will to restore an operational naval air force was strong. The Americans agreed to supply aircraft to rebuild the naval air arm (*Aéronautique Navale*) even though this branch was not seen as a priority compared to the patrol aircraft able to respond to the U-boat threat, a tasking exclusively given to the Navy in French doctrine.

Via Lend-Lease, while the French Air Force was earmarked to receive 100 A-24Bs, the US supplied a batch of brand-new 36 SBD-5s to the French Navy (BuNos 54565 to 54600); 32 were delivered in March 1944 at Casablanca in French Morocco (54580, 54584, 54588, 54592 and 54594 were believed retained in the US and never delivered; 54544 was possibly a replacement aircraft extracted from US stock to make up the 32). It was enough to equip two bombing squadrons, the 3FB and the 4FB, normally established with 12 aircraft (plus four in reserve), an establishment reached at a later stage. More SBD-5s were supplied, 21 arriving in December 1944 (BuNos 35928, 36106, 36188, 36219, 36224, 36326, 36335, 36357, 36361, 36386, 36553, 36655, 36730, 36743, 36751, 36756, 36757, 36761, 36817, 54382 and 54418), all being new or with low airframe hours. At least one other, 28931, was delivered from USN stocks in April 1945. In all, it seems that, during the war, 58 SBD-5s were supplied to the French, but not all were new. Navy personnel were drafted from former twin-engine units previously flying Martin 167 and LeO 45 bombers, disbanded for the purpose. Commanded by *Lieutenant de Vaisseau* F. Ortolan (3FB) and *Lieutenant de Vaisseau* R. Béhic (4FB), and under the supervision of USN instructors, training began at once at Agadir. For the USN, the units were known as VFB-1 and VFB-2 respectively. It was a long process as the French had not only to master modern aircraft but also Allied tactics and procedures, and the English language. Training was plagued with various accidents, the first taking place on 21 July 1944, then on 19 August, both involving 3FB and causing the death of the crew on each occasion.

By September, the two French bomber squadrons had become operational within Fleet Air Wing 15. This was a large operational force tasked to control the sea frontier area of Morocco, flying over the Atlantic coast in search of German U-boats with US Navy PB4Y Liberators and PV-1 Venturas, and the two recently operational French PBY Catalina units. A detachment of 3FB was sent to Port Lyautey on 21 September where some convoy escorts and coastal patrols were carried out, initially with a daily average rate of six sorties, soon reduced to four by mid-October, then two by 2 November. For the French, however, it was time to use

Above: A line-up of French Navy SBDs. In the foreground is SBD-5 '154' (BuNo 54573) of the 3FB.

Left: Armourers fixing cluster bombs to racks at Cognac. Note the underwing French roundel with the anchor; the fuselage roundel did not have this nautical feature.

Above: A formation of SBD-5s during a training flight, with '167'/BuNo 36760 leading '171'/BuNo 54575 and '174'/BuNo 54586 in 1945. They belonged to the 4FB.
Below: SBD '166'/BuNo 54574 of the 4FB leading another formation.

the two units in combat. It took time to eventually find a place where the Dauntlesses could be used on operations. In the autumn of 1944, some strongpoints around the French ports on the Atlantic coast in France still held out, obliging the Allies to deploy ground units to take care of them. Some air support was needed, but the USAAF was heavily engaged against the Germans in the eastern part of France. Therefore, it was decided that, as the two French units were available, they would be deployed to provide air support in those areas; the one selected was near the port of Bordeaux. It was not what the French naval flyers had wished for, hoping to be embarked on board a ship again someday, but it was action anyway. The 3FB made the move on 23 November, followed by the 4FB the next day to form a provisional wing, commanded by Capitaine de Corvette F Lainé. The first sorties were flown on 9 December, the target being a train hidden under a bridge near La Rochelle. Six SBDs of the 3FB took off to discover the train had gone. The bridge was attacked but a strong wind pushed the bombs away and the results were poor; all bombs missed the target. More missions were carried out over the next few days and the first losses were recorded. On 14 December, an SBD from 4FB was hit while attacking a flak position at Verdon and was obliged to make a forced landing between the lines. Soon after, on 23 December, the provisional wing became GAN 2 (*Groupe Aéronaval n°2*), still under the command of Lainé. At the end of December, GAN 2 had carried out 199 sorties and dropped 85 tons of bombs.

The New Year started badly for the French who lost an aircraft of 4FB. The 1000-lb bomb did not release correctly and the crew, *Officier des Equipages* P. Goffeny and *Quartier-Maître* M. Chauvin, could not recover and were killed. Another SBD was lost with its crew (*Maître* V. Gérold and *Quartier-Maître* A. Guenanen) to flak on 18 February. In March, replacement crews began to arrive; a few local flights were carried out before sending them on operations. It was during one such flight on the 22nd that an SBD crashed in the Pauillac area, causing the death of *Second Maître* Y. Abgrall and *Quartier-Maître* C. Hague. In April, the rhythm of the sorties intensified as the strongpoint shrunk progressively. No less than 246 tons of bombs were dropped in 444 sorties, but this came with a cost. On 16 April, *Maître* L Bonnefoy and *Second Maître* F. Bataille of 3FB were shot down and killed near Royan. This pocket of resistance held out until the last day of the European war so the Allies continued to bomb the area. On 8 May, the day of the German surrender, two SDBs of 3FB collided during their dives, causing one to crash near Dampierre. Neither of the two crewmen, *Maître* J. Auradou and *Second Maître* M. Lebrun, survived. A few hours later, the war was over. From 9 December, the group had performed more than 1,100 sorties and dropped 532 tons of bombs. Five SBDs were lost to enemy fire or written off to various causes while based in France; four crews perished in action.

With the war now over in Europe, the French Navy continued to rebuild its naval air arm around an aircraft carrier; at least another three SBDs drawn from USN stocks were taken on charge during the summer: 36334, 36558, 54563. A former Royal Navy aircraft carrier, HMS *Biter*, albeit in poor condition, was handed over to the French on 9 April 1945 and would become the first French carrier of the post-war period. It was renamed *Dixmude*. It was joined in August by *Arromanches* (ex-HMS *Colossus*). In June, the GAN 2 moved to the naval base at Hyères on the French Mediterranean coast where training continued. On 24 August, during a night practice flight, two SBDs collided on landing, one landing on the other. One crew member was killed and both aircraft were only good for scrapping.

The SBD continued to be the backbone of French naval bomber squadrons, 3FB and 4FB being renamed 3.F and 4.F from 1 January 1946. Both units would complete a tour of operations over French Indochina embarked on the recently acquired aircraft carrier. Indeed, an insurrection in French Indochina had risen in December 1946. Even though combat intensity was low early on, four SBDs were lost to various causes during their cruise, the last one ending in January 1949. Obsolete and war weary, the type was eventually withdrawn from use in November.

SBD-5 '167'/BuNo 36730, with 16 bomb markings, seen during a training flight. After the war, this SBD remained with 4FB, was re-coded '4.F-7' and served until March 1948 when it was stricken.

Summary of the aircraft lost on Operations - French 3.FB & 4.FB

Date	Pilot	S/N	Unit	Serial	Code	Fate
01.01.45	OE2 Paul **Goffeny**		4.FB	**54544**	176	†
	QM Michel **Chauvin**		4.FB			†
18.02.45	PM Vincent **Gérold**		4.FB	**54581**	173	†
	QM André **Guénanen**		4.FB			†
16.04.45	Mt Louis **Bonnefoy**		3.FB	**54577**	158	†
	SM François **Bataille**		3.FB			†
08.05.45	Mt Jaques **Auradou**		3.FB	**54576**	144	†
	SM Marcel **Lebrun**		3.FB			†

Total: 4

SBD-5 '169'/BuNo 36817 with 30 bomb markings returning from a sortie. Note the rear gun installed, a weapon that was really not needed as the Luftwaffe, besides nighttime supply drops, was absent from the area. This aircraft was lost in an accident on 24.08.45 but using another code.

Summary of the aircraft lost by accident - French 3.FB & 4.FB

Date	Pilot	S/N	Unit	Serial	Code	Fate
21.07.44	LV Damien **Morfouace**		3.FB	**54600**		†
	SM Pierre **Sionne**		3.FB			†
19.08.44	EV1 Louis **Spetz**		3.FB	**54598**	172	†
	QM Maurice **Chéreau**		3.FB			†
22.03.45	SM Yves **Abgrall**		3.FB	**54599**	150	†
	QM Carlos **Hague**		3.FB			†
24.08.45	Mt Denis **Noblet**		3.FB	**36817**		†
	?					-
	?		3.FB	**54572**		-
	?					-

Total: 5

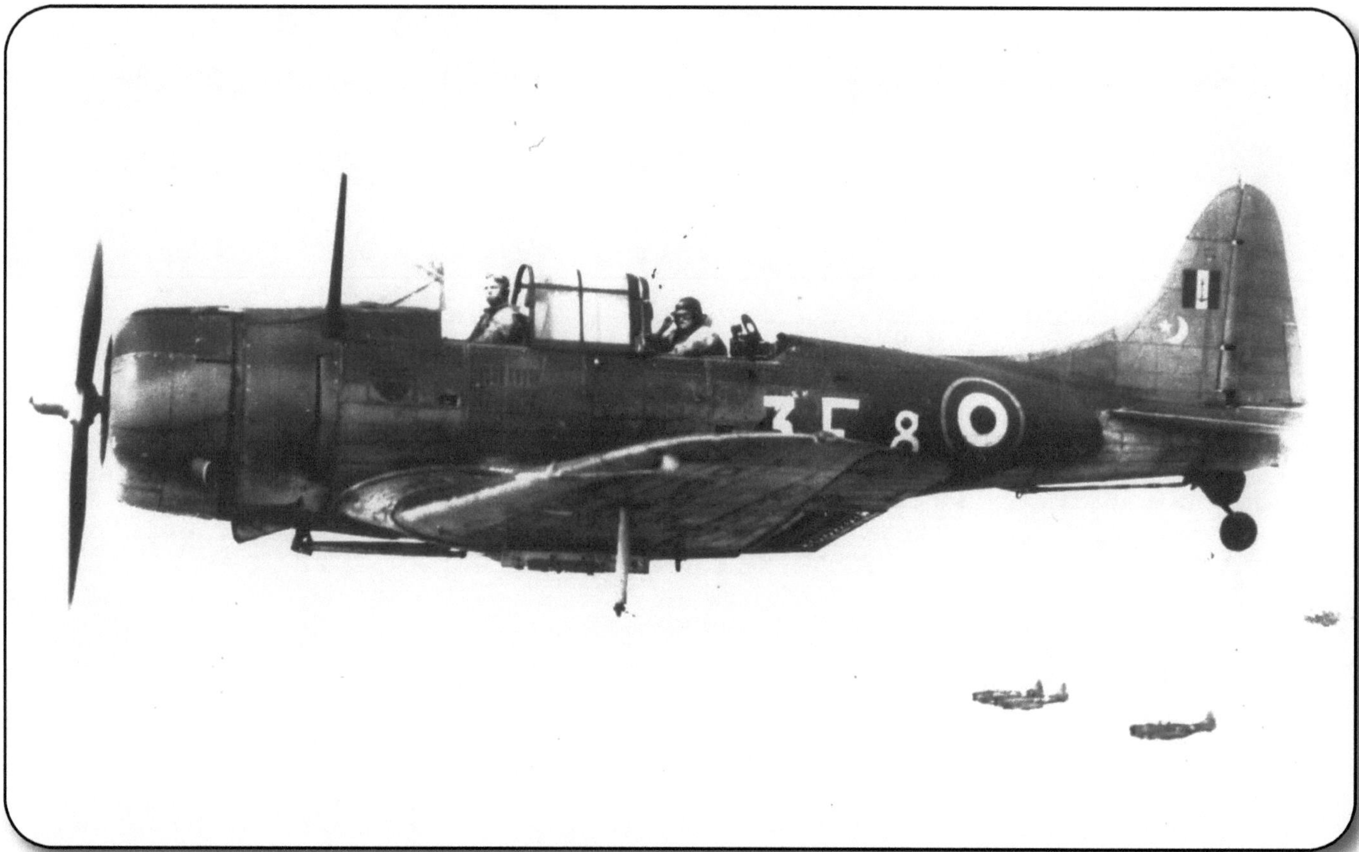

Some scenes of French SBDs after the war in France and in Indochina wearing the new system of codes.

Above: SBD '3.F-8' of *Flottille 3F*, the first unit to be engaged in Indochina.
Below: SBD '3.F-4' being launched from the aircraft carrier *Arromanches*.

Above, two SBDs of *Flottille* 4F flying over Morocco in 1947.
Below, SBD '4.F.5' of *Flottille* 4F on patrol over southern Indochina with the waters of the Mekong in the background.

Douglas SBD-5 NZ5057
No. 25 Squadron RNZAF
Squadron Leader T.J. McL. de Lange / Flying Officer L.T. Sewell
Henderson Field, Guadalcanal (Solomon Islands), March 1944

Douglas SBD-5 167/BuNo 36730
Flotille 4.FB
Cognac, (France), winter 44-45

SQUADRONS! - The series

Donald James Matthew BLAKESLEE DFC

Supermarine Spitfire Mk.VB EN951
No. 133 (Eagle) Squadron
Flight Lieutenant D. J. M. Blakeslee
CAN/ J.4351
Gravesend (UK), August 1942

Charles Cuthbertson LEARMONTH DFC

Douglas Boston Mk. III A28-6 (ex-AL893)
No. 22 Squadron RAAF
Squadron Leader C. C. Learmonth
402,383
Port Moresby (New Guinea), spring 1943

Hans Anton MAURENBRECHER

Curtiss P-40N-35-CU C3-560
No. 120 (NEI) Squadron
Major H. Maurenbrecher
Biak (New Guinea), 1943-1944

Roland Prosper BEAMONT DSO* DFC*

Hawker Tempest Mk.V FN751
No. 150 Wing
Wing Commander R. P. Beamont
RAF No. 41801
Bradwell Bay (UK), April 1944

Ronald Thomas SUSANS DSO DFC

North American P-51D-25-NT A68-724
No. 77 squadron, RAAF
Squadron Leader R. T. Susans
O/4330
Bofu (Japan), 1947

James Henry LACEY DFM*

Supermarine Spitfire Mk.XIV RN135
No. 17 Squadron
Squadron Leader J. H. Lacey
RAF No. 112799
Seletar (Singapore), octomber 1945

Introducing's RAF In Combat and Bravo Bravo Aviation's collection of
highly-detailed and historically accurate, high-quality aviation prints.
For more information on available prints, please visit :

www.RAF-IN-COMBAT.com   or   BRAVO BRAVO AVIATION
BBA
HIGH QUALITY AVIATION ILLUSTRATION
WWW.BravoBravoAviation.COM

Print available for this book:

PL-088 - T.J.M. DE LANGE

Theodore Jasper Maclean DE LANGE DFC

Douglas SBD-5 NZ5057
No. 25 Squadron RNZAF
Squadron Leader T. J. Macl. de Lange
NZ4060
Henderson Field, Guadalcanal (Solomon Islands)
March 1944